SHARKS SET II

BASKING SHARKS

Adam G. Klein
ABDO Publishing Company

visit us at
www.abdopub.com

Published by ABDO Publishing Company, 4940 Viking Drive, Edina, Minnesota 55435.
Copyright © 2006 by Abdo Consulting Group, Inc. International copyrights reserved in all
countries. No part of this book may be reproduced in any form without written permission from
the publisher. The Checkerboard Library™ is a trademark and logo of ABDO Publishing
Company.

Printed in the United States.

Cover Photo: Corbis
Interior Photos: Corbis pp. 11, 15; Dan Burton / www.underwaterimages.co.uk pp. 9, 19; Getty
    Images p. 16; © Howard Hall / SeaPics.com p. 5; © Jonathan Bird / SeaPics.com p. 13; ©
    Ron & Valerie Taylor / SeaPics.com p. 17; © Tom Campbell / SeaPics.com p. 21; Uko Gorter
    pp. 6-7

Series Coordinator: Heidi M. Dahmes
Editors: Heidi M. Dahmes, Megan M. Gunderson
Art Direction: Neil Klinepier

Library of Congress Cataloging-in-Publication Data

Klein, Adam G., 1976-
    Basking sharks / Adam G. Klein.
        p. cm. -- (Sharks. Set II)
    Includes bibliographical references.
    ISBN 1-59679-285-X
    1. Basking shark--Juvenile literature. I. Title.

QL638.95.C37K58 2005
597.3--dc22

                                                                    2005046900

CONTENTS

BASKING SHARKS AND FAMILY

There are many creatures swimming through the oceans of the world. They come in all sizes and countless species. Many can be harmful if they are disrespected. But, few are more feared than the shark.

There are about 275 species of sharks, but they all share common features. Sharks are fish made of **cartilage** rather than bone. They are **predatory** creatures. And, most are **carnivores**.

The basking shark is truly one of the masters of the sea. It is the second-largest fish in the world. Few animals try to challenge this massive sea monster.

Even with all of its strength, the basking shark is a very gentle creature. Basking sharks prefer to just glide through the ocean. They feast on **plankton** and bask in the sun.

The basking shark is also known as the bone shark, the elephant shark, and the sailfish shark.

What They Look Like

Basking sharks can be identified by their grayish brown color. Their bodies are long and **cylindrical**. They have a pointy snout, big eyes, and many rows of small teeth. All of these features make a distinct creature. But, there is one definite way to identify a basking shark.

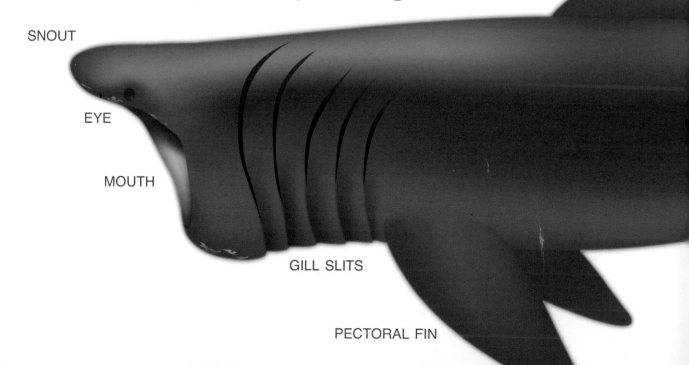

SNOUT

EYE

MOUTH

GILL SLITS

PECTORAL FIN

Basking sharks are the second-biggest fish in the world. They can get up to 46 feet (14 m) long. And, they can weigh almost 18 tons (16 t)! The average basking shark is 32 feet (10 m) long and weighs up to six tons (5 t). At that size, their mouths are about three feet (1 m) wide.

Another unusual feature of the basking shark is its broad gills. A basking shark's gill slits almost completely surround its head. They are used for breathing. And, they assist in eating.

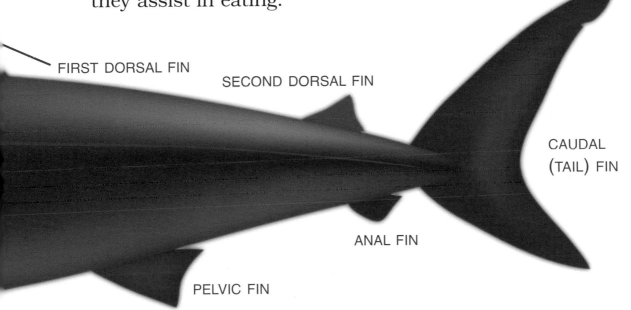

FIRST DORSAL FIN

SECOND DORSAL FIN

CAUDAL (TAIL) FIN

ANAL FIN

PELVIC FIN

WHERE THEY LIVE

Basking sharks live in **temperate** and cold waters worldwide. They **migrate** with the seasons. These sharks travel thousands of miles because of the water temperature and the availability of food.

Basking sharks move at a slow three miles per hour (5 km/h). They travel alone or in groups of three to four. But, schools of more than 100 basking sharks have been reported.

Basking sharks can be found at the surface of the ocean. A basking shark cruises along with its back and first **dorsal** fin sticking out of the water. Some people think the sharks look like they are sunning themselves. This is how the basking shark got its name.

A basking shark can also dive very deep. The species has been spotted up to 2,461 feet (750 m) below the surface. This is a big range for a shark to live in.

When temperatures are warmer, basking sharks migrate north. In cooler months, they go south.

FOOD

Basking sharks do not usually hunt for a meal. Instead, they swim through the water with their mouths open. As they swim, small fish, **plankton**, **larvae**, and other creatures collect in the shark's massive mouth.

This food gets caught in the shark's gill rakers. The gill rakers strain the food from the water. And, the water is pushed out through the gills. A basking shark's gill rakers filter about 2,000 tons (1,800 t) of water per hour.

In the winter, the basking shark sheds its gill rakers. What happens to the shark while it regrows its gill rakers is mostly unknown. Some people think that the shark lives off of fat stored in its **liver**. Others believe that the shark looks for food at the bottom of the ocean.

Still, the shark survives until the gill rakers grow back. After regrowth, the shark returns to the surface to bask again.

Gill rakers are bristles similar to teeth that are inside the gill slits. These gill rakers filter the basking shark's food from the water.

SENSES

A shark needs to figure out its surroundings while traveling. Sharks have well-developed eyesight. But, they use their senses of smell and hearing more often. This is especially true over long distances and while hunting.

Sharks use their sense of smell to identify objects. **Odorants** wash into a shark's nasal sac and tell the shark what is around it.

There is one sense that is unique to sharks and their relatives. Sharks have small **pores** on their bodies called ampullae of Lorenzini. These pores sense electrical fields in the water. All living creatures produce an electrical charge. Sharks use the ampullae of Lorenzini to locate their prey.

A basking shark

BABIES

Little is known about how a basking shark reproduces. When a female shark is between 12 and 16 years old, she is ready for children. After mating, eggs inside the female become fertilized. Basking sharks are believed to carry their young for about three years.

Basking sharks are either **ovoviviparous** or **viviparous**. The mother carries her young inside of her while they develop. The **embryos** survive until birth by feeding off of the remaining eggs and other unborn sharks. This is called oophagy.

When it is time, the mother shark will birth one to two pups. When they are born, the pups swim away. They are fully developed and ready to care for themselves.

Basking shark pups are the largest fish babies in the world. They can be six feet (2 m) long at birth! Like many large shark species, basking sharks grow very slowly. It takes many years for a basking shark to reach its full size.

Often when a female shark is ready to give birth, she enters a nursery area. This is to keep her pups safe from larger sharks.

ATTACK AND DEFENSE

Few animals would even try to hunt a basking shark because of its great size. But, this does not mean that they are always safe. In many countries, people hunt basking sharks. They are killed for their oil, fins, skin, and meat.

A basking shark's fins are used for shark fin soup. Its **liver** is used for oil. The basking shark's liver accounts for about 25 percent of its total weight and is very valuable.

Humans are not the basking shark's only enemy. Orcas and tiger sharks feed on basking sharks.

Sharks are hunted for their fins. Some fishers cut the fins off and throw the sharks back in the ocean.

In colonial times, the oil was used in oil lamps. Today, there are many uses for shark oil but most are medicinal purposes.

Basking sharks also have to deal with **parasites**. Sea lampreys use basking sharks for transportation. These fishlike creatures attach themselves to the shark's skin and are an annoyance. Sometimes, people see basking sharks leap out of the water to shake off parasites.

ATTACKS ON HUMANS

Despite its massive size, the basking shark is a gentle creature. This good-natured shark is tolerant of divers. It will sometimes inspect a boat out of curiosity. But, it will not attack unless **harpooned**.

In 1808, a basking shark was mistaken for a sea monster. This was before scientific knowledge of these great creatures was available. A large sea snake was reported to have washed up on the Isle of Stronsa in the British Isles.

The next year, a man named Everard Home read the story in a paper. Home had studied sharks and came to the conclusion that the monster was actually a basking shark.

Finally in 1933, Professor James Ritchie wrote a paper agreeing with Home. The mystery of the sea monster was solved.

The basking shark is still a mysterious creature even though scientists are able to study this shark up close.

BASKING SHARK FACTS

Scientific Name:

Basking shark   *Cetorhinus maximus*

Average Size:

32 feet (10 m) long and weighs up to six tons (5 t)
A basking shark pup can be six feet (2 m) long at
birth.

Where They're Found:

In temperate and cold waters worldwide. Basking
sharks live in the northern and mild areas of the
Atlantic, Pacific, and Indian oceans.

Sharks are covered in toothlike scales called dermal denticles. These denticles serve as a protective cover for the skin.

GLOSSARY

carnivore - an animal or plant that eats meat.

cartilage (KAHR-tuh-lihj) - the soft, elastic connective tissue in the skeleton. A person's nose and ears are made of cartilage.

cylindrical - having the shape of two parallel circles bound by a curved surface.

dorsal - located near or on the back, especially of an animal.

embryo - an organism in the early stages of development.

harpoon - to strike or kill with a weapon resembling a spear that has a rope attached to it.

larva - the early form of an animal, such as a frog, that must change before it is in its adult form.

liver - a large organ that produces bile, stores carbohydrates, and performs other bodily functions.

migrate - to move from one place to another, often to find food.

odorant - a fragrant substance.

ovoviviparous (OH-voh-veye-VIH-puh-ruhs) - a fish or reptile that carries its eggs inside it while they develop.

parasite - an organism that lives off of another organism of a different species.

plankton - small animals and plants that float in a body of water.

pore - a small opening in an animal or plant through which matter passes.

predator - an animal that kills and eats other animals.

temperate - having neither very hot nor very cold weather.

viviparous (veye-VIH-puh-ruhs) - an animal that produces live young instead of eggs from within the body.

WEB SITES

To learn more about basking sharks, visit ABDO Publishing Company on the World Wide Web at **www.abdopub.com**. Web sites about basking sharks are featured on our Book Links page. These links are routinely monitored and updated to provide the most current information available.

INDEX